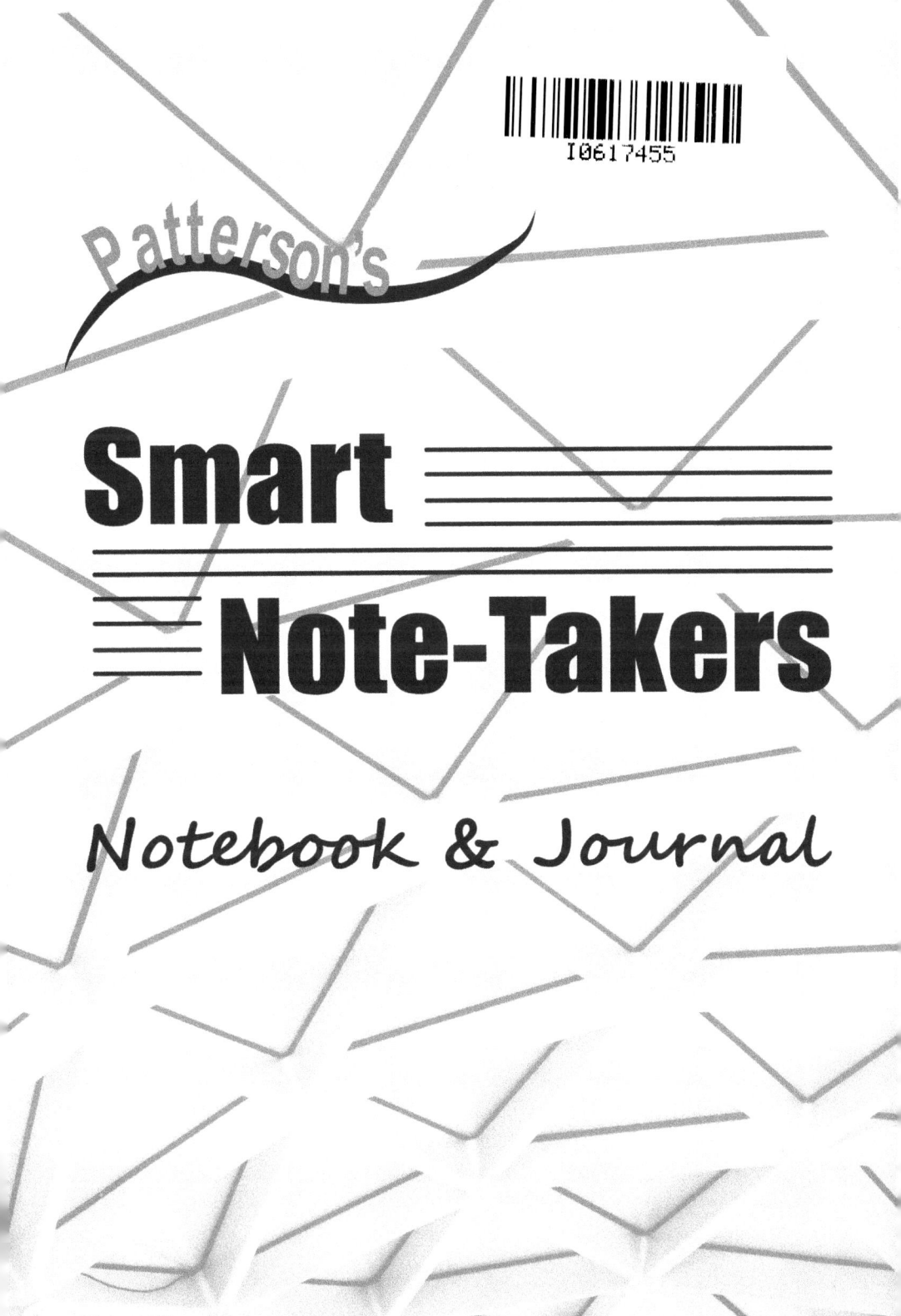

Patterson's

Smart
Note-Takers

Notebook & Journal

I0617455

Each line in the notebook has a unique number for easy reference

4A _Saul was the ch_

4B _Where did he g_

4C _it was that time_

just in time bec

Easily tie notes together from other lines and pages

swers to that question. 4B

less you kept reading.

a surprise to everyone.

Easily organize your pages by showing where to continue for the same topic

☐ Continued on next page
☒ Continued on page _____12_____
☐ End

Smart Note-Takers

Notebook & Journal

Patterson's Smart Note-Takers
Evolution Publication LLC

This belongs to:

_____

Date: _____ Reference: _____

Title: _____

1A _____ ⋮ ____

1B _____ ⋮ ____

1C _____ ⋮ ____

1D _____ ⋮ ____

1E _____ ⋮ ____

1F _____ ⋮ ____

1G _____ ⋮ ____

1H _____ ⋮ ____

1I _____ ⋮ ____

1J _____ ⋮ ____

1K _____ ⋮ ____

1L _____ ⋮ ____

1M _____ ⋮ ____

1N _____ ⋮ ____

1O _____ ⋮ ____

1P _____ ⋮ ____

1Q _____ ⋮ ____

1R _____ ⋮ ____

1S _____ ⋮ ____

1T _____ ⋮ ____

1U _____ ⋮ ____

1V _____ ⋮ ____

☐ Continued on next page
☐ Continued on page _____
☐ End

Date: _____   Reference: _____

Title: _____

Ref. Line

2A _____ ⋮ _____

2B _____ ⋮ _____

2C _____ ⋮ _____

2D _____ ⋮ _____

2E _____ ⋮ _____

2F _____ ⋮ _____

2G _____ ⋮ _____

2H _____ ⋮ _____

2I _____ ⋮ _____

2J _____ ⋮ _____

2K _____ ⋮ _____

2L _____ ⋮ _____

2M _____ ⋮ _____

2N _____ ⋮ _____

2O _____ ⋮ _____

2P _____ ⋮ _____

2Q _____ ⋮ _____

2R _____ ⋮ _____

2S _____ ⋮ _____

2T _____ ⋮ _____

2U _____ ⋮ _____

2V _____ ⋮ _____

☐ Continued on next page
☐ Continued on page _____
☐ End

‖ 2

Date: _____　　　Reference: _____

Title: _____

3A _____ : _____

3B _____ : _____

3C _____ : _____

3D _____ : _____

3E _____ : _____

3F _____ : _____

3G _____ : _____

3H _____ : _____

3I _____ : _____

3J _____ : _____

3K _____ : _____

3L _____ : _____

3M _____ : _____

3N _____ : _____

3O _____ : _____

3P _____ : _____

3Q _____ : _____

3R _____ : _____

3S _____ : _____

3T _____ : _____

3U _____ : _____

3V _____ : _____

☐ Continued on next page
☐ Continued on page _____
☐ End

‖ 3

Date: _____   Reference: _____

Title: _____

Ref. Line

4A _____ ⋮ _____

4B _____ ⋮ _____

4C _____ ⋮ _____

4D _____ ⋮ _____

4E _____ ⋮ _____

4F _____ ⋮ _____

4G _____ ⋮ _____

4H _____ ⋮ _____

4I _____ ⋮ _____

4J _____ ⋮ _____

4K _____ ⋮ _____

4L _____ ⋮ _____

4M _____ ⋮ _____

4N _____ ⋮ _____

4O _____ ⋮ _____

4P _____ ⋮ _____

4Q _____ ⋮ _____

4R _____ ⋮ _____

4S _____ ⋮ _____

4T _____ ⋮ _____

4U _____ ⋮ _____

4V _____ ⋮ _____

☐ Continued on next page
☐ Continued on page _____
☐ End

4

Date: _____   Reference: _____

Title: _____

Ref. Line

5A _____

5B _____

5C _____

5D _____

5E _____

5F _____

5G _____

5H _____

5I _____

5J _____

5K _____

5L _____

5M _____

5N _____

5O _____

5P _____

5Q _____

5R _____

5S _____

5T _____

5U _____

5V _____

☐ Continued on next page
☐ Continued on page _____
☐ End

‖   5

Date: _____   Reference: _____

Title: _____

6A _____ ⋮ _____

6B _____ ⋮ _____

6C _____ ⋮ _____

6D _____ ⋮ _____

6E _____ ⋮ _____

6F _____ ⋮ _____

6G _____ ⋮ _____

6H _____ ⋮ _____

6I _____ ⋮ _____

6J _____ ⋮ _____

6K _____ ⋮ _____

6L _____ ⋮ _____

6M _____ ⋮ _____

6N _____ ⋮ _____

6O _____ ⋮ _____

6P _____ ⋮ _____

6Q _____ ⋮ _____

6R _____ ⋮ _____

6S _____ ⋮ _____

6T _____ ⋮ _____

6U _____ ⋮ _____

6V _____ ⋮ _____

☐ Continued on next page
☐ Continued on page _____
☐ End

‖   6

Date: _____   Reference: _____

Title: _____

Ref. Line

7A _____ :_____

7B _____ :_____

7C _____ :_____

7D _____ :_____

7E _____ :_____

7F _____ :_____

7G _____ :_____

7H _____ :_____

7I _____ :_____

7J _____ :_____

7K _____ :_____

7L _____ :_____

7M _____ :_____

7N _____ :_____

7O _____ :_____

7P _____ :_____

7Q _____ :_____

7R _____ :_____

7S _____ :_____

7T _____ :_____

7U _____ :_____

7V _____ :_____

☐ Continued on next page
☐ Continued on page _____
☐ End

7

Date: _____   Reference: _____

Title: _____

8A _____ __.____

8B _____ __.____

8C _____ __.____

8D _____ __.____

8E _____ __.____

8F _____ __.____

8G _____ __.____

8H _____ __.____

8I _____ __.____

8J _____ __.____

8K _____ __.____

8L _____ __.____

8M _____ __.____

8N _____ __.____

8O _____ __.____

8P _____ __.____

8Q _____ __.____

8R _____ __.____

8S _____ __.____

8T _____ __.____

8U _____ __.____

8V _____ __.____

☐ Continued on next page
☐ Continued on page _____
☐ End

Date: _____   Reference: _____

Title: _____

Ref. Line

9A _____ ⋮ _____

9B _____ ⋮ _____

9C _____ ⋮ _____

9D _____ ⋮ _____

9E _____ ⋮ _____

9F _____ ⋮ _____

9G _____ ⋮ _____

9H _____ ⋮ _____

9I _____ ⋮ _____

9J _____ ⋮ _____

9K _____ ⋮ _____

9L _____ ⋮ _____

9M _____ ⋮ _____

9N _____ ⋮ _____

9O _____ ⋮ _____

9P _____ ⋮ _____

9Q _____ ⋮ _____

9R _____ ⋮ _____

9S _____ ⋮ _____

9T _____ ⋮ _____

9U _____ ⋮ _____

9V _____ ⋮ _____

☐ Continued on next page
☐ Continued on page _____
☐ End

9

Date: _____   Reference: _____

Title: _____

Ref. Line

10A _____ : _____

10B _____ : _____

10C _____ : _____

10D _____ : _____

10E _____ : _____

10F _____ : _____

10G _____ : _____

10H _____ : _____

10I _____ : _____

10J _____ : _____

10K _____ : _____

10L _____ : _____

10M _____ : _____

10N _____ : _____

10O _____ : _____

10P _____ : _____

10Q _____ : _____

10R _____ : _____

10S _____ : _____

10T _____ : _____

10U _____ : _____

10V _____ : _____

☐ Continued on next page
☐ Continued on page _____
☐ End

Date: _____   Reference: _____

Title: _____

Ref. Line

11A _____ ⋮____

11B _____ ⋮____

11C _____ ⋮____

11D _____ ⋮____

11E _____ ⋮____

11F _____ ⋮____

11G _____ ⋮____

11H _____ ⋮____

11I _____ ⋮____

11J _____ ⋮____

11K _____ ⋮____

11L _____ ⋮____

11M _____ ⋮____

11N _____ ⋮____

11O _____ ⋮____

11P _____ ⋮____

11Q _____ ⋮____

11R _____ ⋮____

11S _____ ⋮____

11T _____ ⋮____

11U _____ ⋮____

11V _____ ⋮____

☐ Continued on next page
☐ Continued on page _____
☐ End

Date: _____ Reference: _____

Title: _____

Ref. Line

12A _____ : _____

12B _____ : _____

12C _____ : _____

12D _____ : _____

12E _____ : _____

12F _____ : _____

12G _____ : _____

12H _____ : _____

12I _____ : _____

12J _____ : _____

12K _____ : _____

12L _____ : _____

12M _____ : _____

12N _____ : _____

12O _____ : _____

12P _____ : _____

12Q _____ : _____

12R _____ : _____

12S _____ : _____

12T _____ : _____

12U _____ : _____

12V _____ : _____

☐ Continued on next page
☐ Continued on page _____
☐ End

Date: _____ Reference: _____

Title: _____

Ref. Line

13A _____ : ____

13B _____ : ____

13C _____ : ____

13D _____ : ____

13E _____ : ____

13F _____ : ____

13G _____ : ____

13H _____ : ____

13I _____ : ____

13J _____ : ____

13K _____ : ____

13L _____ : ____

13M _____ : ____

13N _____ : ____

13O _____ : ____

13P _____ : ____

13Q _____ : ____

13R _____ : ____

13S _____ : ____

13T _____ : ____

13U _____ : ____

13V _____ : ____

☐ Continued on next page
☐ Continued on page _____
☐ End

Date: _____   Reference: _____

Title: _____

Ref. Line

14A _____ : _____

14B _____ : _____

14C _____ : _____

14D _____ : _____

14E _____ : _____

14F _____ : _____

14G _____ : _____

14H _____ : _____

14I _____ : _____

14J _____ : _____

14K _____ : _____

14L _____ : _____

14M _____ : _____

14N _____ : _____

14O _____ : _____

14P _____ : _____

14Q _____ : _____

14R _____ : _____

14S _____ : _____

14T _____ : _____

14U _____ : _____

14V _____ : _____

☐ Continued on next page
☐ Continued on page _____
☐ End

Date: _____   Reference: _____

Title: _____

15A _____ ⋮ _____

15B _____ ⋮ _____

15C _____ ⋮ _____

15D _____ ⋮ _____

15E _____ ⋮ _____

15F _____ ⋮ _____

15G _____ ⋮ _____

15H _____ ⋮ _____

15I _____ ⋮ _____

15J _____ ⋮ _____

15K _____ ⋮ _____

15L _____ ⋮ _____

15M _____ ⋮ _____

15N _____ ⋮ _____

15O _____ ⋮ _____

15P _____ ⋮ _____

15Q _____ ⋮ _____

15R _____ ⋮ _____

15S _____ ⋮ _____

15T _____ ⋮ _____

15U _____ ⋮ _____

15V _____ ⋮ _____

☐ Continued on next page
☐ Continued on page _____
☐ End

Date: _____   Reference: _____

Title: _____

Ref. Line

16A _____ ⋮ _____

16B _____ ⋮ _____

16C _____ ⋮ _____

16D _____ ⋮ _____

16E _____ ⋮ _____

16F _____ ⋮ _____

16G _____ ⋮ _____

16H _____ ⋮ _____

16I _____ ⋮ _____

16J _____ ⋮ _____

16K _____ ⋮ _____

16L _____ ⋮ _____

16M _____ ⋮ _____

16N _____ ⋮ _____

16O _____ ⋮ _____

16P _____ ⋮ _____

16Q _____ ⋮ _____

16R _____ ⋮ _____

16S _____ ⋮ _____

16T _____ ⋮ _____

16U _____ ⋮ _____

16V _____ ⋮ _____

☐ Continued on next page
☐ Continued on page _____
☐ End

Date: _____ Reference: _____

Title: _____

Ref. Line

17A _____ ⋮ _____

17B _____ ⋮ _____

17C _____ ⋮ _____

17D _____ ⋮ _____

17E _____ ⋮ _____

17F _____ ⋮ _____

17G _____ ⋮ _____

17H _____ ⋮ _____

17I _____ ⋮ _____

17J _____ ⋮ _____

17K _____ ⋮ _____

17L _____ ⋮ _____

17M _____ ⋮ _____

17N _____ ⋮ _____

17O _____ ⋮ _____

17P _____ ⋮ _____

17Q _____ ⋮ _____

17R _____ ⋮ _____

17S _____ ⋮ _____

17T _____ ⋮ _____

17U _____ ⋮ _____

17V _____ ⋮ _____

☐ Continued on next page
☐ Continued on page _____
☐ End

Date: _____ Reference: _____

Title: _____

Ref. Line

18A _____ . _____

18B _____ . _____

18C _____ . _____

18D _____ . _____

18E _____ . _____

18F _____ . _____

18G _____ . _____

18H _____ . _____

18I _____ . _____

18J _____ . _____

18K _____ . _____

18L _____ . _____

18M _____ . _____

18N _____ . _____

18O _____ . _____

18P _____ . _____

18Q _____ . _____

18R _____ . _____

18S _____ . _____

18T _____ . _____

18U _____ . _____

18V _____ . _____

☐ Continued on next page
☐ Continued on page _____
☐ End

‖ 18

Date: _____   Reference: _____

Title: _____

Ref. Line

19A _____ :_____

19B _____ :_____

19C _____ :_____

19D _____ :_____

19E _____ :_____

19F _____ :_____

19G _____ :_____

19H _____ :_____

19I _____ :_____

19J _____ :_____

19K _____ :_____

19L _____ :_____

19M _____ :_____

19N _____ :_____

19O _____ :_____

19P _____ :_____

19Q _____ :_____

19R _____ :_____

19S _____ :_____

19T _____ :_____

19U _____ :_____

19V _____ :_____

☐ Continued on next page
☐ Continued on page _____
☐ End

Date: _____ Reference: _____

Title: _____

Ref. Line

20A _____ : _____

20B _____ : _____

20C _____ : _____

20D _____ : _____

20E _____ : _____

20F _____ : _____

20G _____ : _____

20H _____ : _____

20I _____ : _____

20J _____ : _____

20K _____ : _____

20L _____ : _____

20M _____ : _____

20N _____ : _____

20O _____ : _____

20P _____ : _____

20Q _____ : _____

20R _____ : _____

20S _____ : _____

20T _____ : _____

20U _____ : _____

20V _____ : _____

☐ Continued on next page
☐ Continued on page _____
☐ End

Date: _____   Reference: _____

Title: _____

Ref. Line

21A _____ : _____

21B _____ : _____

21C _____ : _____

21D _____ : _____

21E _____ : _____

21F _____ : _____

21G _____ : _____

21H _____ : _____

21I _____ : _____

21J _____ : _____

21K _____ : _____

21L _____ : _____

21M _____ : _____

21N _____ : _____

21O _____ : _____

21P _____ : _____

21Q _____ : _____

21R _____ : _____

21S _____ : _____

21T _____ : _____

21U _____ : _____

21V _____ : _____

☐ Continued on next page
☐ Continued on page _____
☐ End

Date: _____   Reference: _____

Title: _____

Ref. Line

22A _____ :_____

22B _____ :_____

22C _____ :_____

22D _____ :_____

22E _____ :_____

22F _____ :_____

22G _____ :_____

22H _____ :_____

22I _____ :_____

22J _____ :_____

22K _____ :_____

22L _____ :_____

22M _____ :_____

22N _____ :_____

22O _____ :_____

22P _____ :_____

22Q _____ :_____

22R _____ :_____

22S _____ :_____

22T _____ :_____

22U _____ :_____

22V _____ :_____

☐ Continued on next page
☐ Continued on page _____
☐ End

Date: _____   Reference: _____

Title: _____

Ref. Line

23A _____ : _____

23B _____ : _____

23C _____ : _____

23D _____ : _____

23E _____ : _____

23F _____ : _____

23G _____ : _____

23H _____ : _____

23I _____ : _____

23J _____ : _____

23K _____ : _____

23L _____ : _____

23M _____ : _____

23N _____ : _____

23O _____ : _____

23P _____ : _____

23Q _____ : _____

23R _____ : _____

23S _____ : _____

23T _____ : _____

23U _____ : _____

23V _____ : _____

☐ Continued on next page
☐ Continued on page _____
☐ End

23

Date: _____   Reference: _____

Title: _____

Ref. Line

24A _____ ⋮ _____

24B _____ ⋮ _____

24C _____ ⋮ _____

24D _____ ⋮ _____

24E _____ ⋮ _____

24F _____ ⋮ _____

24G _____ ⋮ _____

24H _____ ⋮ _____

24I _____ ⋮ _____

24J _____ ⋮ _____

24K _____ ⋮ _____

24L _____ ⋮ _____

24M _____ ⋮ _____

24N _____ ⋮ _____

24O _____ ⋮ _____

24P _____ ⋮ _____

24Q _____ ⋮ _____

24R _____ ⋮ _____

24S _____ ⋮ _____

24T _____ ⋮ _____

24U _____ ⋮ _____

24V _____ ⋮ _____

☐ Continued on next page
☐ Continued on page _____
☐ End

‖ 24

Date: _____ Reference: _____

Title: _____

Ref. Line

25A _____ : _____

25B _____ : _____

25C _____ : _____

25D _____ : _____

25E _____ : _____

25F _____ : _____

25G _____ : _____

25H _____ : _____

25I _____ : _____

25J _____ : _____

25K _____ : _____

25L _____ : _____

25M _____ : _____

25N _____ : _____

25O _____ : _____

25P _____ : _____

25Q _____ : _____

25R _____ : _____

25S _____ : _____

25T _____ : _____

25U _____ : _____

25V _____ : _____

☐ Continued on next page
☐ Continued on page _____
☐ End

25

Date: _____ Reference: _____

Title: _____

26A _____ : _____

26B _____ : _____

26C _____ : _____

26D _____ : _____

26E _____ : _____

26F _____ : _____

26G _____ : _____

26H _____ : _____

26I _____ : _____

26J _____ : _____

26K _____ : _____

26L _____ : _____

26M _____ : _____

26N _____ : _____

26O _____ : _____

26P _____ : _____

26Q _____ : _____

26R _____ : _____

26S _____ : _____

26T _____ : _____

26U _____ : _____

26V _____ : _____

☐ Continued on next page
☐ Continued on page _____
☐ End

Date: _____   Reference: _____

Title: _____

Ref. Line

27A _____ ____ : ____

27B _____ ____ : ____

27C _____ ____ : ____

27D _____ ____ : ____

27E _____ ____ : ____

27F _____ ____ : ____

27G _____ ____ : ____

27H _____ ____ : ____

27I _____ ____ : ____

27J _____ ____ : ____

27K _____ ____ : ____

27L _____ ____ : ____

27M _____ ____ : ____

27N _____ ____ : ____

27O _____ ____ : ____

27P _____ ____ : ____

27Q _____ ____ : ____

27R _____ ____ : ____

27S _____ ____ : ____

27T _____ ____ : ____

27U _____ ____ : ____

27V _____ ____ : ____

☐ Continued on next page
☐ Continued on page _____
☐ End

‖ 27

Date: _____ Reference: _____

Title: _____

Ref. Line

28A _____ ⋮ _____

28B _____ ⋮ _____

28C _____ ⋮ _____

28D _____ ⋮ _____

28E _____ ⋮ _____

28F _____ ⋮ _____

28G _____ ⋮ _____

28H _____ ⋮ _____

28I _____ ⋮ _____

28J _____ ⋮ _____

28K _____ ⋮ _____

28L _____ ⋮ _____

28M _____ ⋮ _____

28N _____ ⋮ _____

28O _____ ⋮ _____

28P _____ ⋮ _____

28Q _____ ⋮ _____

28R _____ ⋮ _____

28S _____ ⋮ _____

28T _____ ⋮ _____

28U _____ ⋮ _____

28V _____ ⋮ _____

☐ Continued on next page
☐ Continued on page _____
☐ End

Date: _____ Reference: _____

Title: _____

Ref. Line

29A _____

29B _____

29C _____

29D _____

29E _____

29F _____

29G _____

29H _____

29I _____

29J _____

29K _____

29L _____

29M _____

29N _____

29O _____

29P _____

29Q _____

29R _____

29S _____

29T _____

29U _____

29V _____

☐ Continued on next page
☐ Continued on page _____
☐ End

|| 29

Date: _____ Reference: _____

Title: _____

Ref. Line

30A _____ ⋮ _____

30B _____ ⋮ _____

30C _____ ⋮ _____

30D _____ ⋮ _____

30E _____ ⋮ _____

30F _____ ⋮ _____

30G _____ ⋮ _____

30H _____ ⋮ _____

30I _____ ⋮ _____

30J _____ ⋮ _____

30K _____ ⋮ _____

30L _____ ⋮ _____

30M _____ ⋮ _____

30N _____ ⋮ _____

30O _____ ⋮ _____

30P _____ ⋮ _____

30Q _____ ⋮ _____

30R _____ ⋮ _____

30S _____ ⋮ _____

30T _____ ⋮ _____

30U _____ ⋮ _____

30V _____ ⋮ _____

☐ Continued on next page
☐ Continued on page _____
☐ End

Date: _____   Reference: _____

Title: _____

Ref. Line

31A _____ ⋮ _____

31B _____ ⋮ _____

31C _____ ⋮ _____

31D _____ ⋮ _____

31E _____ ⋮ _____

31F _____ ⋮ _____

31G _____ ⋮ _____

31H _____ ⋮ _____

31I _____ ⋮ _____

31J _____ ⋮ _____

31K _____ ⋮ _____

31L _____ ⋮ _____

31M _____ ⋮ _____

31N _____ ⋮ _____

31O _____ ⋮ _____

31P _____ ⋮ _____

31Q _____ ⋮ _____

31R _____ ⋮ _____

31S _____ ⋮ _____

31T _____ ⋮ _____

31U _____ ⋮ _____

31V _____ ⋮ _____

☐ Continued on next page
☐ Continued on page _____
☐ End

Date: _____   Reference: _____

Title: _____

32A _____ : _____

32B _____ : _____

32C _____ : _____

32D _____ : _____

32E _____ : _____

32F _____ : _____

32G _____ : _____

32H _____ : _____

32I _____ : _____

32J _____ : _____

32K _____ : _____

32L _____ : _____

32M _____ : _____

32N _____ : _____

32O _____ : _____

32P _____ : _____

32Q _____ : _____

32R _____ : _____

32S _____ : _____

32T _____ : _____

32U _____ : _____

32V _____ : _____

☐ Continued on next page
☐ Continued on page _____
☐ End

‖ 32

Date: _____   Reference: _____

Title: _____

Ref. Line

33A _____:_____

33B _____:_____

33C _____:_____

33D _____:_____

33E _____:_____

33F _____:_____

33G _____:_____

33H _____:_____

33I _____:_____

33J _____:_____

33K _____:_____

33L _____:_____

33M _____:_____

33N _____:_____

33O _____:_____

33P _____:_____

33Q _____:_____

33R _____:_____

33S _____:_____

33T _____:_____

33U _____:_____

33V _____:_____

☐ Continued on next page
☐ Continued on page _____
☐ End

‖ 33

Date: _____   Reference: _____

Title: _____

Ref. Line

34A _____ : _____

34B _____ : _____

34C _____ : _____

34D _____ : _____

34E _____ : _____

34F _____ : _____

34G _____ : _____

34H _____ : _____

34I _____ : _____

34J _____ : _____

34K _____ : _____

34L _____ : _____

34M _____ : _____

34N _____ : _____

34O _____ : _____

34P _____ : _____

34Q _____ : _____

34R _____ : _____

34S _____ : _____

34T _____ : _____

34U _____ : _____

34V _____ : _____

☐ Continued on next page
☐ Continued on page _____
☐ End

Date: _____ Reference: _____

Title: _____

Ref. Line

35A _____ : _____

35B _____ : _____

35C _____ : _____

35D _____ : _____

35E _____ : _____

35F _____ : _____

35G _____ : _____

35H _____ : _____

35I _____ : _____

35J _____ : _____

35K _____ : _____

35L _____ : _____

35M _____ : _____

35N _____ : _____

35O _____ : _____

35P _____ : _____

35Q _____ : _____

35R _____ : _____

35S _____ : _____

35T _____ : _____

35U _____ : _____

35V _____ : _____

☐ Continued on next page
☐ Continued on page _____
☐ End

Date: _____   Reference: _____

Title: _____

Ref. Line

36A _____ ⋮ _____

36B _____ ⋮ _____

36C _____ ⋮ _____

36D _____ ⋮ _____

36E _____ ⋮ _____

36F _____ ⋮ _____

36G _____ ⋮ _____

36H _____ ⋮ _____

36I _____ ⋮ _____

36J _____ ⋮ _____

36K _____ ⋮ _____

36L _____ ⋮ _____

36M _____ ⋮ _____

36N _____ ⋮ _____

36O _____ ⋮ _____

36P _____ ⋮ _____

36Q _____ ⋮ _____

36R _____ ⋮ _____

36S _____ ⋮ _____

36T _____ ⋮ _____

36U _____ ⋮ _____

36V _____ ⋮ _____

☐ Continued on next page
☐ Continued on page _____
☐ End

‖ 36

Date: _____ Reference: _____

Title: _____

Ref. Line

37A _____ : _____

37B _____ : _____

37C _____ : _____

37D _____ : _____

37E _____ : _____

37F _____ : _____

37G _____ : _____

37H _____ : _____

37I _____ : _____

37J _____ : _____

37K _____ : _____

37L _____ : _____

37M _____ : _____

37N _____ : _____

37O _____ : _____

37P _____ : _____

37Q _____ : _____

37R _____ : _____

37S _____ : _____

37T _____ : _____

37U _____ : _____

37V _____ : _____

☐ Continued on next page
☐ Continued on page _____
☐ End

Date: _____   Reference: _____

Title: _____

Ref. Line

38A _____ :_____

38B _____ :_____

38C _____ :_____

38D _____ :_____

38E _____ :_____

38F _____ :_____

38G _____ :_____

38H _____ :_____

38I _____ :_____

38J _____ :_____

38K _____ :_____

38L _____ :_____

38M _____ :_____

38N _____ :_____

38O _____ :_____

38P _____ :_____

38Q _____ :_____

38R _____ :_____

38S _____ :_____

38T _____ :_____

38U _____ :_____

38V _____ :_____

☐ Continued on next page
☐ Continued on page _____
☐ End

‖ 38

Date: _____   Reference: _____

Title: _____

39A _____

39B _____

39C _____

39D _____

39E _____

39F _____

39G _____

39H _____

39I _____

39J _____

39K _____

39L _____

39M _____

39N _____

39O _____

39P _____

39Q _____

39R _____

39S _____

39T _____

39U _____

39V _____

☐ Continued on next page
☐ Continued on page _____
☐ End

Date: _____   Reference: _____

Title: _____

Ref. Line

40A _____ : _____

40B _____ : _____

40C _____ : _____

40D _____ : _____

40E _____ : _____

40F _____ : _____

40G _____ : _____

40H _____ : _____

40I _____ : _____

40J _____ : _____

40K _____ : _____

40L _____ : _____

40M _____ : _____

40N _____ : _____

40O _____ : _____

40P _____ : _____

40Q _____ : _____

40R _____ : _____

40S _____ : _____

40T _____ : _____

40U _____ : _____

40V _____ : _____

☐ Continued on next page
☐ Continued on page _____
☐ End

Date: _____   Reference: _____

Title: _____

Ref. Line

41A _____ : _____

41B _____ : _____

41C _____ : _____

41D _____ : _____

41E _____ : _____

41F _____ : _____

41G _____ : _____

41H _____ : _____

41I _____ : _____

41J _____ : _____

41K _____ : _____

41L _____ : _____

41M _____ : _____

41N _____ : _____

41O _____ : _____

41P _____ : _____

41Q _____ : _____

41R _____ : _____

41S _____ : _____

41T _____ : _____

41U _____ : _____

41V _____ : _____

☐ Continued on next page
☐ Continued on page _____
☐ End

Date: _____   Reference: _____

Title: _____

Ref. Line

42A _____ : _____

42B _____ : _____

42C _____ : _____

42D _____ : _____

42E _____ : _____

42F _____ : _____

42G _____ : _____

42H _____ : _____

42I _____ : _____

42J _____ : _____

42K _____ : _____

42L _____ : _____

42M _____ : _____

42N _____ : _____

42O _____ : _____

42P _____ : _____

42Q _____ : _____

42R _____ : _____

42S _____ : _____

42T _____ : _____

42U _____ : _____

42V _____ : _____

☐ Continued on next page
☐ Continued on page _____
☐ End

|| 42

Date: _____ Reference: _____

Title: _____

Ref. Line

43A _____ ⋮ _____

43B _____ ⋮ _____

43C _____ ⋮ _____

43D _____ ⋮ _____

43E _____ ⋮ _____

43F _____ ⋮ _____

43G _____ ⋮ _____

43H _____ ⋮ _____

43I _____ ⋮ _____

43J _____ ⋮ _____

43K _____ ⋮ _____

43L _____ ⋮ _____

43M _____ ⋮ _____

43N _____ ⋮ _____

43O _____ ⋮ _____

43P _____ ⋮ _____

43Q _____ ⋮ _____

43R _____ ⋮ _____

43S _____ ⋮ _____

43T _____ ⋮ _____

43U _____ ⋮ _____

43V _____ ⋮ _____

☐ Continued on next page
☐ Continued on page _____
☐ End

‖ 43

Date: _____   Reference: _____

Title: _____

Ref. Line

44A _____ : _____

44B _____ : _____

44C _____ : _____

44D _____ : _____

44E _____ : _____

44F _____ : _____

44G _____ : _____

44H _____ : _____

44I _____ : _____

44J _____ : _____

44K _____ : _____

44L _____ : _____

44M _____ : _____

44N _____ : _____

44O _____ : _____

44P _____ : _____

44Q _____ : _____

44R _____ : _____

44S _____ : _____

44T _____ : _____

44U _____ : _____

44V _____ : _____

☐ Continued on next page
☐ Continued on page _____
☐ End

Date: _____ Reference: _____

Title: _____

45A _____

45B _____

45C _____

45D _____

45E _____

45F _____

45G _____

45H _____

45I _____

45J _____

45K _____

45L _____

45M _____

45N _____

45O _____

45P _____

45Q _____

45R _____

45S _____

45T _____

45U _____

45V _____

☐ Continued on next page
☐ Continued on page _____
☐ End

Date: _____   Reference: _____

Title: _____

Ref. Line

46A _____ : _____

46B _____ : _____

46C _____ : _____

46D _____ : _____

46E _____ : _____

46F _____ : _____

46G _____ : _____

46H _____ : _____

46I _____ : _____

46J _____ : _____

46K _____ : _____

46L _____ : _____

46M _____ : _____

46N _____ : _____

46O _____ : _____

46P _____ : _____

46Q _____ : _____

46R _____ : _____

46S _____ : _____

46T _____ : _____

46U _____ : _____

46V _____ : _____

☐ Continued on next page
☐ Continued on page _____
☐ End

Date: _____ Reference: _____

Title: _____

Ref. Line

47A _____ ⋮ ____

47B _____ ⋮ ____

47C _____ ⋮ ____

47D _____ ⋮ ____

47E _____ ⋮ ____

47F _____ ⋮ ____

47G _____ ⋮ ____

47H _____ ⋮ ____

47I _____ ⋮ ____

47J _____ ⋮ ____

47K _____ ⋮ ____

47L _____ ⋮ ____

47M _____ ⋮ ____

47N _____ ⋮ ____

47O _____ ⋮ ____

47P _____ ⋮ ____

47Q _____ ⋮ ____

47R _____ ⋮ ____

47S _____ ⋮ ____

47T _____ ⋮ ____

47U _____ ⋮ ____

47V _____ ⋮ ____

☐ Continued on next page
☐ Continued on page _____
☐ End

‖ 47

Date: _____   Reference: _____

Title: _____

48A _____ ⋮ _____

48B _____ ⋮ _____

48C _____ ⋮ _____

48D _____ ⋮ _____

48E _____ ⋮ _____

48F _____ ⋮ _____

48G _____ ⋮ _____

48H _____ ⋮ _____

48I _____ ⋮ _____

48J _____ ⋮ _____

48K _____ ⋮ _____

48L _____ ⋮ _____

48M _____ ⋮ _____

48N _____ ⋮ _____

48O _____ ⋮ _____

48P _____ ⋮ _____

48Q _____ ⋮ _____

48R _____ ⋮ _____

48S _____ ⋮ _____

48T _____ ⋮ _____

48U _____ ⋮ _____

48V _____ ⋮ _____

☐ Continued on next page
☐ Continued on page _____
☐ End

Date: _____   Reference: _____

Title: _____

Ref. Line

49A _____ ⋮ _____

49B _____ ⋮ _____

49C _____ ⋮ _____

49D _____ ⋮ _____

49E _____ ⋮ _____

49F _____ ⋮ _____

49G _____ ⋮ _____

49H _____ ⋮ _____

49I _____ ⋮ _____

49J _____ ⋮ _____

49K _____ ⋮ _____

49L _____ ⋮ _____

49M _____ ⋮ _____

49N _____ ⋮ _____

49O _____ ⋮ _____

49P _____ ⋮ _____

49Q _____ ⋮ _____

49R _____ ⋮ _____

49S _____ ⋮ _____

49T _____ ⋮ _____

49U _____ ⋮ _____

49V _____ ⋮ _____

☐ Continued on next page
☐ Continued on page _____
☐ End

|| 49

Date: _____   Reference: _____

Title: _____

Ref. Line

50A _____ : _____

50B _____ : _____

50C _____ : _____

50D _____ : _____

50E _____ : _____

50F _____ : _____

50G _____ : _____

50H _____ : _____

50I _____ : _____

50J _____ : _____

50K _____ : _____

50L _____ : _____

50M _____ : _____

50N _____ : _____

50O _____ : _____

50P _____ : _____

50Q _____ : _____

50R _____ : _____

50S _____ : _____

50T _____ : _____

50U _____ : _____

50V _____ : _____

☐ Continued on next page
☐ Continued on page _____
☐ End

‖ 50

Date: _____   Reference: _____

Title: _____

Ref. Line

51A _____ : _____

51B _____ : _____

51C _____ : _____

51D _____ : _____

51E _____ : _____

51F _____ : _____

51G _____ : _____

51H _____ : _____

51I _____ : _____

51J _____ : _____

51K _____ : _____

51L _____ : _____

51M _____ : _____

51N _____ : _____

51O _____ : _____

51P _____ : _____

51Q _____ : _____

51R _____ : _____

51S _____ : _____

51T _____ : _____

51U _____ : _____

51V _____ : _____

☐ Continued on next page
☐ Continued on page _____
☐ End

Date: _____ Reference: _____

Title: _____

Ref. Line

52A _____ ⋮ _____

52B _____ ⋮ _____

52C _____ ⋮ _____

52D _____ ⋮ _____

52E _____ ⋮ _____

52F _____ ⋮ _____

52G _____ ⋮ _____

52H _____ ⋮ _____

52I _____ ⋮ _____

52J _____ ⋮ _____

52K _____ ⋮ _____

52L _____ ⋮ _____

52M _____ ⋮ _____

52N _____ ⋮ _____

52O _____ ⋮ _____

52P _____ ⋮ _____

52Q _____ ⋮ _____

52R _____ ⋮ _____

52S _____ ⋮ _____

52T _____ ⋮ _____

52U _____ ⋮ _____

52V _____ ⋮ _____

☐ Continued on next page
☐ Continued on page _____
☐ End

|| 52

Date: _____   Reference: _____

Title: _____

Ref. Line

53A _____⋮_____

53B _____⋮_____

53C _____⋮_____

53D _____⋮_____

53E _____⋮_____

53F _____⋮_____

53G _____⋮_____

53H _____⋮_____

53I _____⋮_____

53J _____⋮_____

53K _____⋮_____

53L _____⋮_____

53M _____⋮_____

53N _____⋮_____

53O _____⋮_____

53P _____⋮_____

53Q _____⋮_____

53R _____⋮_____

53S _____⋮_____

53T _____⋮_____

53U _____⋮_____

53V _____⋮_____

☐ Continued on next page
☐ Continued on page _____
☐ End

Date: _____   Reference: _____

Title: _____

54A _____ ⋮ _____

54B _____ ⋮ _____

54C _____ ⋮ _____

54D _____ ⋮ _____

54E _____ ⋮ _____

54F _____ ⋮ _____

54G _____ ⋮ _____

54H _____ ⋮ _____

54I _____ ⋮ _____

54J _____ ⋮ _____

54K _____ ⋮ _____

54L _____ ⋮ _____

54M _____ ⋮ _____

54N _____ ⋮ _____

54O _____ ⋮ _____

54P _____ ⋮ _____

54Q _____ ⋮ _____

54R _____ ⋮ _____

54S _____ ⋮ _____

54T _____ ⋮ _____

54U _____ ⋮ _____

54V _____ ⋮ _____

☐ Continued on next page
☐ Continued on page _____
☐ End

Date: _____   Reference: _____

Title: _____

Ref. Line

55A _____ : _____

55B _____ : _____

55C _____ : _____

55D _____ : _____

55E _____ : _____

55F _____ : _____

55G _____ : _____

55H _____ : _____

55I _____ : _____

55J _____ : _____

55K _____ : _____

55L _____ : _____

55M _____ : _____

55N _____ : _____

55O _____ : _____

55P _____ : _____

55Q _____ : _____

55R _____ : _____

55S _____ : _____

55T _____ : _____

55U _____ : _____

55V _____ : _____

☐ Continued on next page
☐ Continued on page _____
☐ End

|| 55

Date: _____   Reference: _____

Title: _____

Ref. Line

56A _____ : _____

56B _____ : _____

56C _____ : _____

56D _____ : _____

56E _____ : _____

56F _____ : _____

56G _____ : _____

56H _____ : _____

56I _____ : _____

56J _____ : _____

56K _____ : _____

56L _____ : _____

56M _____ : _____

56N _____ : _____

56O _____ : _____

56P _____ : _____

56Q _____ : _____

56R _____ : _____

56S _____ : _____

56T _____ : _____

56U _____ : _____

56V _____ : _____

☐ Continued on next page
☐ Continued on page _____
☐ End

‖ 56

Date: _____   Reference: _____

Title: _____

Ref. Line

57A _____ :_____

57B _____ :_____

57C _____ :_____

57D _____ :_____

57E _____ :_____

57F _____ :_____

57G _____ :_____

57H _____ :_____

57I _____ :_____

57J _____ :_____

57K _____ :_____

57L _____ :_____

57M _____ :_____

57N _____ :_____

57O _____ :_____

57P _____ :_____

57Q _____ :_____

57R _____ :_____

57S _____ :_____

57T _____ :_____

57U _____ :_____

57V _____ :_____

☐ Continued on next page
☐ Continued on page _____
☐ End

Date: _____   Reference: _____

Title: _____

Ref. Line

58A _____ : _____

58B _____ : _____

58C _____ : _____

58D _____ : _____

58E _____ : _____

58F _____ : _____

58G _____ : _____

58H _____ : _____

58I _____ : _____

58J _____ : _____

58K _____ : _____

58L _____ : _____

58M _____ : _____

58N _____ : _____

58O _____ : _____

58P _____ : _____

58Q _____ : _____

58R _____ : _____

58S _____ : _____

58T _____ : _____

58U _____ : _____

58V _____ : _____

☐ Continued on next page
☐ Continued on page _____
☐ End

Date: _____   Reference: _____

Title: _____

Ref. Line

59A _____ : _____

59B _____ : _____

59C _____ : _____

59D _____ : _____

59E _____ : _____

59F _____ : _____

59G _____ : _____

59H _____ : _____

59I _____ : _____

59J _____ : _____

59K _____ : _____

59L _____ : _____

59M _____ : _____

59N _____ : _____

59O _____ : _____

59P _____ : _____

59Q _____ : _____

59R _____ : _____

59S _____ : _____

59T _____ : _____

59U _____ : _____

59V _____ : _____

☐ Continued on next page
☐ Continued on page _____
☐ End

Date: _____   Reference: _____

Title: _____

Ref. Line

60A _____ ⋮ _____

60B _____ ⋮ _____

60C _____ ⋮ _____

60D _____ ⋮ _____

60E _____ ⋮ _____

60F _____ ⋮ _____

60G _____ ⋮ _____

60H _____ ⋮ _____

60I _____ ⋮ _____

60J _____ ⋮ _____

60K _____ ⋮ _____

60L _____ ⋮ _____

60M _____ ⋮ _____

60N _____ ⋮ _____

60O _____ ⋮ _____

60P _____ ⋮ _____

60Q _____ ⋮ _____

60R _____ ⋮ _____

60S _____ ⋮ _____

60T _____ ⋮ _____

60U _____ ⋮ _____

60V _____ ⋮ _____

☐ Continued on next page
☐ Continued on page _____
☐ End

Date: _____   Reference: _____

Title: _____

Ref. Line

61A _____

61B _____

61C _____

61D _____

61E _____

61F _____

61G _____

61H _____

61I _____

61J _____

61K _____

61L _____

61M _____

61N _____

61O _____

61P _____

61Q _____

61R _____

61S _____

61T _____

61U _____

61V _____

☐ Continued on next page
☐ Continued on page _____
☐ End

61

Date: _____   Reference: _____

Title: _____

Ref. Line

62A _____ : _____

62B _____ : _____

62C _____ : _____

62D _____ : _____

62E _____ : _____

62F _____ : _____

62G _____ : _____

62H _____ : _____

62I _____ : _____

62J _____ : _____

62K _____ : _____

62L _____ : _____

62M _____ : _____

62N _____ : _____

62O _____ : _____

62P _____ : _____

62Q _____ : _____

62R _____ : _____

62S _____ : _____

62T _____ : _____

62U _____ : _____

62V _____ : _____

☐ Continued on next page
☐ Continued on page _____
☐ End

Date: _____ Reference: _____

Title: _____

Ref. Line

63A _____

63B _____

63C _____

63D _____

63E _____

63F _____

63G _____

63H _____

63I _____

63J _____

63K _____

63L _____

63M _____

63N _____

63O _____

63P _____

63Q _____

63R _____

63S _____

63T _____

63U _____

63V _____

☐ Continued on next page
☐ Continued on page _____
☐ End

Date: _____ Reference: _____

Title: _____

64A _____ : _____

64B _____ : _____

64C _____ : _____

64D _____ : _____

64E _____ : _____

64F _____ : _____

64G _____ : _____

64H _____ : _____

64I _____ : _____

64J _____ : _____

64K _____ : _____

64L _____ : _____

64M _____ : _____

64N _____ : _____

64O _____ : _____

64P _____ : _____

64Q _____ : _____

64R _____ : _____

64S _____ : _____

64T _____ : _____

64U _____ : _____

64V _____ : _____

☐ Continued on next page
☐ Continued on page _____
☐ End

Date: _____   Reference: _____

Title: _____

Ref. Line

65A _____ : _____

65B _____ : _____

65C _____ : _____

65D _____ : _____

65E _____ : _____

65F _____ : _____

65G _____ : _____

65H _____ : _____

65I _____ : _____

65J _____ : _____

65K _____ : _____

65L _____ : _____

65M _____ : _____

65N _____ : _____

65O _____ : _____

65P _____ : _____

65Q _____ : _____

65R _____ : _____

65S _____ : _____

65T _____ : _____

65U _____ : _____

65V _____ : _____

☐ Continued on next page
☐ Continued on page _____
☐ End

Date: _____   Reference: _____

Title: _____

Ref. Line

66A _____ ⋮ _____

66B _____ ⋮ _____

66C _____ ⋮ _____

66D _____ ⋮ _____

66E _____ ⋮ _____

66F _____ ⋮ _____

66G _____ ⋮ _____

66H _____ ⋮ _____

66I _____ ⋮ _____

66J _____ ⋮ _____

66K _____ ⋮ _____

66L _____ ⋮ _____

66M _____ ⋮ _____

66N _____ ⋮ _____

66O _____ ⋮ _____

66P _____ ⋮ _____

66Q _____ ⋮ _____

66R _____ ⋮ _____

66S _____ ⋮ _____

66T _____ ⋮ _____

66U _____ ⋮ _____

66V _____ ⋮ _____

☐ Continued on next page
☐ Continued on page _____
☐ End

Date: _____   Reference: _____

Title: _____

Ref. Line

67A _____ : _____

67B _____ : _____

67C _____ : _____

67D _____ : _____

67E _____ : _____

67F _____ : _____

67G _____ : _____

67H _____ : _____

67I _____ : _____

67J _____ : _____

67K _____ : _____

67L _____ : _____

67M _____ : _____

67N _____ : _____

67O _____ : _____

67P _____ : _____

67Q _____ : _____

67R _____ : _____

67S _____ : _____

67T _____ : _____

67U _____ : _____

67V _____ : _____

☐ Continued on next page
☐ Continued on page _____
☐ End

Date: _____   Reference: _____

Title: _____

Ref. Line

68A _____ : _____

68B _____ : _____

68C _____ : _____

68D _____ : _____

68E _____ : _____

68F _____ : _____

68G _____ : _____

68H _____ : _____

68I _____ : _____

68J _____ : _____

68K _____ : _____

68L _____ : _____

68M _____ : _____

68N _____ : _____

68O _____ : _____

68P _____ : _____

68Q _____ : _____

68R _____ : _____

68S _____ : _____

68T _____ : _____

68U _____ : _____

68V _____ : _____

☐ Continued on next page
☐ Continued on page _____
☐ End

‖ 68

Date: _____   Reference: _____

Title: _____

Ref. Line

69A _____ ⋮_____

69B _____ ⋮_____

69C _____ ⋮_____

69D _____ ⋮_____

69E _____ ⋮_____

69F _____ ⋮_____

69G _____ ⋮_____

69H _____ ⋮_____

69I _____ ⋮_____

69J _____ ⋮_____

69K _____ ⋮_____

69L _____ ⋮_____

69M _____ ⋮_____

69N _____ ⋮_____

69O _____ ⋮_____

69P _____ ⋮_____

69Q _____ ⋮_____

69R _____ ⋮_____

69S _____ ⋮_____

69T _____ ⋮_____

69U _____ ⋮_____

69V _____ ⋮_____

☐ Continued on next page
☐ Continued on page _____
☐ End

69

Date: _____   Reference: _____

Title: _____

Ref. Line

70A _____ ⋮ _____

70B _____ ⋮ _____

70C _____ ⋮ _____

70D _____ ⋮ _____

70E _____ ⋮ _____

70F _____ ⋮ _____

70G _____ ⋮ _____

70H _____ ⋮ _____

70I _____ ⋮ _____

70J _____ ⋮ _____

70K _____ ⋮ _____

70L _____ ⋮ _____

70M _____ ⋮ _____

70N _____ ⋮ _____

70O _____ ⋮ _____

70P _____ ⋮ _____

70Q _____ ⋮ _____

70R _____ ⋮ _____

70S _____ ⋮ _____

70T _____ ⋮ _____

70U _____ ⋮ _____

70V _____ ⋮ _____

☐ Continued on next page
☐ Continued on page _____
☐ End

|| 70

Date: _____   Reference: _____

Title: _____

Ref. Line

71A _____ : _____

71B _____ : _____

71C _____ : _____

71D _____ : _____

71E _____ : _____

71F _____ : _____

71G _____ : _____

71H _____ : _____

71I _____ : _____

71J _____ : _____

71K _____ : _____

71L _____ : _____

71M _____ : _____

71N _____ : _____

71O _____ : _____

71P _____ : _____

71Q _____ : _____

71R _____ : _____

71S _____ : _____

71T _____ : _____

71U _____ : _____

71V _____ : _____

☐ Continued on next page
☐ Continued on page _____
☐ End

Date: _____   Reference: _____

Title: _____

Ref. Line

72A _____ _____

72B _____ _____

72C _____ _____

72D _____ _____

72E _____ _____

72F _____ _____

72G _____ _____

72H _____ _____

72I _____ _____

72J _____ _____

72K _____ _____

72L _____ _____

72M _____ _____

72N _____ _____

72O _____ _____

72P _____ _____

72Q _____ _____

72R _____ _____

72S _____ _____

72T _____ _____

72U _____ _____

72V _____ _____

☐ Continued on next page
☐ Continued on page _____
☐ End

|| 72

Date: _____ Reference: _____

Title: _____

Ref. Line

73A _____ ⋮ _____

73B _____ ⋮ _____

73C _____ ⋮ _____

73D _____ ⋮ _____

73E _____ ⋮ _____

73F _____ ⋮ _____

73G _____ ⋮ _____

73H _____ ⋮ _____

73I _____ ⋮ _____

73J _____ ⋮ _____

73K _____ ⋮ _____

73L _____ ⋮ _____

73M _____ ⋮ _____

73N _____ ⋮ _____

73O _____ ⋮ _____

73P _____ ⋮ _____

73Q _____ ⋮ _____

73R _____ ⋮ _____

73S _____ ⋮ _____

73T _____ ⋮ _____

73U _____ ⋮ _____

73V _____ ⋮ _____

☐ Continued on next page
☐ Continued on page _____
☐ End

Date: _____   Reference: _____

Title: _____

Ref. Line

74A _____ ⋮ _____

74B _____ ⋮ _____

74C _____ ⋮ _____

74D _____ ⋮ _____

74E _____ ⋮ _____

74F _____ ⋮ _____

74G _____ ⋮ _____

74H _____ ⋮ _____

74I _____ ⋮ _____

74J _____ ⋮ _____

74K _____ ⋮ _____

74L _____ ⋮ _____

74M _____ ⋮ _____

74N _____ ⋮ _____

74O _____ ⋮ _____

74P _____ ⋮ _____

74Q _____ ⋮ _____

74R _____ ⋮ _____

74S _____ ⋮ _____

74T _____ ⋮ _____

74U _____ ⋮ _____

74V _____ ⋮ _____

☐ Continued on next page
☐ Continued on page _____
☐ End

‖ 74

Date: _____   Reference: _____

Title: _____

Ref. Line

75A _____ : _____

75B _____ : _____

75C _____ : _____

75D _____ : _____

75E _____ : _____

75F _____ : _____

75G _____ : _____

75H _____ : _____

75I _____ : _____

75J _____ : _____

75K _____ : _____

75L _____ : _____

75M _____ : _____

75N _____ : _____

75O _____ : _____

75P _____ : _____

75Q _____ : _____

75R _____ : _____

75S _____ : _____

75T _____ : _____

75U _____ : _____

75V _____ : _____

☐ Continued on next page
☐ Continued on page _____
☐ End

75

Date: _____   Reference: _____
Title: _____

Ref. Line

76A _____ ⋮ _____

76B _____ ⋮ _____

76C _____ ⋮ _____

76D _____ ⋮ _____

76E _____ ⋮ _____

76F _____ ⋮ _____

76G _____ ⋮ _____

76H _____ ⋮ _____

76I _____ ⋮ _____

76J _____ ⋮ _____

76K _____ ⋮ _____

76L _____ ⋮ _____

76M _____ ⋮ _____

76N _____ ⋮ _____

76O _____ ⋮ _____

76P _____ ⋮ _____

76Q _____ ⋮ _____

76R _____ ⋮ _____

76S _____ ⋮ _____

76T _____ ⋮ _____

76U _____ ⋮ _____

76V _____ ⋮ _____

☐ Continued on next page
☐ Continued on page _____
☐ End

Date: _____   Reference: _____

Title: _____

Ref. Line

77A _____ ⋮ _____

77B _____ ⋮ _____

77C _____ ⋮ _____

77D _____ ⋮ _____

77E _____ ⋮ _____

77F _____ ⋮ _____

77G _____ ⋮ _____

77H _____ ⋮ _____

77I _____ ⋮ _____

77J _____ ⋮ _____

77K _____ ⋮ _____

77L _____ ⋮ _____

77M _____ ⋮ _____

77N _____ ⋮ _____

77O _____ ⋮ _____

77P _____ ⋮ _____

77Q _____ ⋮ _____

77R _____ ⋮ _____

77S _____ ⋮ _____

77T _____ ⋮ _____

77U _____ ⋮ _____

77V _____ ⋮ _____

☐ Continued on next page
☐ Continued on page _____
☐ End

Date: _____   Reference: _____

Title: _____

78A _____ ⋮ _____

78B _____ ⋮ _____

78C _____ ⋮ _____

78D _____ ⋮ _____

78E _____ ⋮ _____

78F _____ ⋮ _____

78G _____ ⋮ _____

78H _____ ⋮ _____

78I _____ ⋮ _____

78J _____ ⋮ _____

78K _____ ⋮ _____

78L _____ ⋮ _____

78M _____ ⋮ _____

78N _____ ⋮ _____

78O _____ ⋮ _____

78P _____ ⋮ _____

78Q _____ ⋮ _____

78R _____ ⋮ _____

78S _____ ⋮ _____

78T _____ ⋮ _____

78U _____ ⋮ _____

78V _____ ⋮ _____

☐ Continued on next page
☐ Continued on page _____
☐ End

Date: _____   Reference: _____

Title: _____

Ref. Line

79A _____ ⋮____

79B _____ ⋮____

79C _____ ⋮____

79D _____ ⋮____

79E _____ ⋮____

79F _____ ⋮____

79G _____ ⋮____

79H _____ ⋮____

79I _____ ⋮____

79J _____ ⋮____

79K _____ ⋮____

79L _____ ⋮____

79M _____ ⋮____

79N _____ ⋮____

79O _____ ⋮____

79P _____ ⋮____

79Q _____ ⋮____

79R _____ ⋮____

79S _____ ⋮____

79T _____ ⋮____

79U _____ ⋮____

79V _____ ⋮____

☐ Continued on next page
☐ Continued on page _____
☐ End

Date: _____ Reference: _____

Title: _____

Ref. Line

80A _____ ⋮____

80B _____ ⋮____

80C _____ ⋮____

80D _____ ⋮____

80E _____ ⋮____

80F _____ ⋮____

80G _____ ⋮____

80H _____ ⋮____

80I _____ ⋮____

80J _____ ⋮____

80K _____ ⋮____

80L _____ ⋮____

80M _____ ⋮____

80N _____ ⋮____

80O _____ ⋮____

80P _____ ⋮____

80Q _____ ⋮____

80R _____ ⋮____

80S _____ ⋮____

80T _____ ⋮____

80U _____ ⋮____

80V _____ ⋮____

☐ Continued on next page
☐ Continued on page _____
☐ End

Date: _____ Reference: _____

Title: _____

Ref. Line

81A _____ ⋮ _____

81B _____ ⋮ _____

81C _____ ⋮ _____

81D _____ ⋮ _____

81E _____ ⋮ _____

81F _____ ⋮ _____

81G _____ ⋮ _____

81H _____ ⋮ _____

81I _____ ⋮ _____

81J _____ ⋮ _____

81K _____ ⋮ _____

81L _____ ⋮ _____

81M _____ ⋮ _____

81N _____ ⋮ _____

81O _____ ⋮ _____

81P _____ ⋮ _____

81Q _____ ⋮ _____

81R _____ ⋮ _____

81S _____ ⋮ _____

81T _____ ⋮ _____

81U _____ ⋮ _____

81V _____ ⋮ _____

☐ Continued on next page
☐ Continued on page _____
☐ End

Date: _____   Reference: _____

Title: _____

Ref. Line

82A _____ ⋮ _____

82B _____ ⋮ _____

82C _____ ⋮ _____

82D _____ ⋮ _____

82E _____ ⋮ _____

82F _____ ⋮ _____

82G _____ ⋮ _____

82H _____ ⋮ _____

82I _____ ⋮ _____

82J _____ ⋮ _____

82K _____ ⋮ _____

82L _____ ⋮ _____

82M _____ ⋮ _____

82N _____ ⋮ _____

82O _____ ⋮ _____

82P _____ ⋮ _____

82Q _____ ⋮ _____

82R _____ ⋮ _____

82S _____ ⋮ _____

82T _____ ⋮ _____

82U _____ ⋮ _____

82V _____ ⋮ _____

☐ Continued on next page
☐ Continued on page _____
☐ End

Date: _____   Reference: _____

Title: _____

Ref. Line

83A _____ : _____

83B _____ : _____

83C _____ : _____

83D _____ : _____

83E _____ : _____

83F _____ : _____

83G _____ : _____

83H _____ : _____

83I _____ : _____

83J _____ : _____

83K _____ : _____

83L _____ : _____

83M _____ : _____

83N _____ : _____

83O _____ : _____

83P _____ : _____

83Q _____ : _____

83R _____ : _____

83S _____ : _____

83T _____ : _____

83U _____ : _____

83V _____ : _____

☐ Continued on next page
☐ Continued on page _____
☐ End

Date: _____   Reference: _____

Title: _____

Ref. Line

84A _____ ┊ _____

84B _____ ┊ _____

84C _____ ┊ _____

84D _____ ┊ _____

84E _____ ┊ _____

84F _____ ┊ _____

84G _____ ┊ _____

84H _____ ┊ _____

84I _____ ┊ _____

84J _____ ┊ _____

84K _____ ┊ _____

84L _____ ┊ _____

84M _____ ┊ _____

84N _____ ┊ _____

84O _____ ┊ _____

84P _____ ┊ _____

84Q _____ ┊ _____

84R _____ ┊ _____

84S _____ ┊ _____

84T _____ ┊ _____

84U _____ ┊ _____

84V _____ ┊ _____

☐ Continued on next page
☐ Continued on page _____
☐ End

Date: _____   Reference: _____

Title: _____

Ref. Line

85A _____ :_____

85B _____ :_____

85C _____ :_____

85D _____ :_____

85E _____ :_____

85F _____ :_____

85G _____ :_____

85H _____ :_____

85I _____ :_____

85J _____ :_____

85K _____ :_____

85L _____ :_____

85M _____ :_____

85N _____ :_____

85O _____ :_____

85P _____ :_____

85Q _____ :_____

85R _____ :_____

85S _____ :_____

85T _____ :_____

85U _____ :_____

85V _____ :_____

☐ Continued on next page
☐ Continued on page _____
☐ End

85

Date: _____   Reference: _____

Title: _____

Ref. Line

86A _____ : _____

86B _____ : _____

86C _____ : _____

86D _____ : _____

86E _____ : _____

86F _____ : _____

86G _____ : _____

86H _____ : _____

86I _____ : _____

86J _____ : _____

86K _____ : _____

86L _____ : _____

86M _____ : _____

86N _____ : _____

86O _____ : _____

86P _____ : _____

86Q _____ : _____

86R _____ : _____

86S _____ : _____

86T _____ : _____

86U _____ : _____

86V _____ : _____

☐ Continued on next page
☐ Continued on page _____
☐ End

|| 86

Date: _____   Reference: _____

Title: _____

87A _____ ⋮ _____

87B _____ ⋮ _____

87C _____ ⋮ _____

87D _____ ⋮ _____

87E _____ ⋮ _____

87F _____ ⋮ _____

87G _____ ⋮ _____

87H _____ ⋮ _____

87I _____ ⋮ _____

87J _____ ⋮ _____

87K _____ ⋮ _____

87L _____ ⋮ _____

87M _____ ⋮ _____

87N _____ ⋮ _____

87O _____ ⋮ _____

87P _____ ⋮ _____

87Q _____ ⋮ _____

87R _____ ⋮ _____

87S _____ ⋮ _____

87T _____ ⋮ _____

87U _____ ⋮ _____

87V _____ ⋮ _____

☐ Continued on next page
☐ Continued on page _____
☐ End

Date: _____ Reference: _____

Title: _____

88A _____

88B _____

88C _____

88D _____

88E _____

88F _____

88G _____

88H _____

88I _____

88J _____

88K _____

88L _____

88M _____

88N _____

88O _____

88P _____

88Q _____

88R _____

88S _____

88T _____

88U _____

88V _____

☐ Continued on next page
☐ Continued on page _____
☐ End

Date: _____   Reference: _____

Title: _____

Ref. Line

89A _____ :_____

89B _____ :_____

89C _____ :_____

89D _____ :_____

89E _____ :_____

89F _____ :_____

89G _____ :_____

89H _____ :_____

89I _____ :_____

89J _____ :_____

89K _____ :_____

89L _____ :_____

89M _____ :_____

89N _____ :_____

89O _____ :_____

89P _____ :_____

89Q _____ :_____

89R _____ :_____

89S _____ :_____

89T _____ :_____

89U _____ :_____

89V _____ :_____

☐ Continued on next page
☐ Continued on page _____
☐ End

‖ 89

Date: _____   Reference: _____

Title: _____

Ref. Line

90A _____ :_____

90B _____ :_____

90C _____ :_____

90D _____ :_____

90E _____ :_____

90F _____ :_____

90G _____ :_____

90H _____ :_____

90I _____ :_____

90J _____ :_____

90K _____ :_____

90L _____ :_____

90M _____ :_____

90N _____ :_____

90O _____ :_____

90P _____ :_____

90Q _____ :_____

90R _____ :_____

90S _____ :_____

90T _____ :_____

90U _____ :_____

90V _____ :_____

☐ Continued on next page
☐ Continued on page _____
☐ End

‖ 90

Date: _____   Reference: _____

Title: _____

Ref. Line

91A _____ ⋮ _____

91B _____ ⋮ _____

91C _____ ⋮ _____

91D _____ ⋮ _____

91E _____ ⋮ _____

91F _____ ⋮ _____

91G _____ ⋮ _____

91H _____ ⋮ _____

91I _____ ⋮ _____

91J _____ ⋮ _____

91K _____ ⋮ _____

91L _____ ⋮ _____

91M _____ ⋮ _____

91N _____ ⋮ _____

91O _____ ⋮ _____

91P _____ ⋮ _____

91Q _____ ⋮ _____

91R _____ ⋮ _____

91S _____ ⋮ _____

91T _____ ⋮ _____

91U _____ ⋮ _____

91V _____ ⋮ _____

☐ Continued on next page
☐ Continued on page _____
☐ End

Date: _____   Reference: _____

Title: _____

92A _____ : _____

92B _____ : _____

92C _____ : _____

92D _____ : _____

92E _____ : _____

92F _____ : _____

92G _____ : _____

92H _____ : _____

92I _____ : _____

92J _____ : _____

92K _____ : _____

92L _____ : _____

92M _____ : _____

92N _____ : _____

92O _____ : _____

92P _____ : _____

92Q _____ : _____

92R _____ : _____

92S _____ : _____

92T _____ : _____

92U _____ : _____

92V _____ : _____

☐ Continued on next page
☐ Continued on page _____
☐ End

Date: _____ Reference: _____

Title: _____

Ref. Line

93A _____ :_____

93B _____ :_____

93C _____ :_____

93D _____ :_____

93E _____ :_____

93F _____ :_____

93G _____ :_____

93H _____ :_____

93I _____ :_____

93J _____ :_____

93K _____ :_____

93L _____ :_____

93M _____ :_____

93N _____ :_____

93O _____ :_____

93P _____ :_____

93Q _____ :_____

93R _____ :_____

93S _____ :_____

93T _____ :_____

93U _____ :_____

93V _____ :_____

☐ Continued on next page
☐ Continued on page _____
☐ End

Date: _____   Reference: _____

Title: _____

94A _____ : _____

94B _____ : _____

94C _____ : _____

94D _____ : _____

94E _____ : _____

94F _____ : _____

94G _____ : _____

94H _____ : _____

94I _____ : _____

94J _____ : _____

94K _____ : _____

94L _____ : _____

94M _____ : _____

94N _____ : _____

94O _____ : _____

94P _____ : _____

94Q _____ : _____

94R _____ : _____

94S _____ : _____

94T _____ : _____

94U _____ : _____

94V _____ : _____

☐ Continued on next page
☐ Continued on page _____
☐ End

Date: _____   Reference: _____

Title: _____

Ref. Line

95A _____ : _____

95B _____ : _____

95C _____ : _____

95D _____ : _____

95E _____ : _____

95F _____ : _____

95G _____ : _____

95H _____ : _____

95I _____ : _____

95J _____ : _____

95K _____ : _____

95L _____ : _____

95M _____ : _____

95N _____ : _____

95O _____ : _____

95P _____ : _____

95Q _____ : _____

95R _____ : _____

95S _____ : _____

95T _____ : _____

95U _____ : _____

95V _____ : _____

☐ Continued on next page
☐ Continued on page _____
☐ End

‖ 95

Date: _____ Reference: _____

Title: _____

Ref. Line

96A _____ ⋮ _____

96B _____ ⋮ _____

96C _____ ⋮ _____

96D _____ ⋮ _____

96E _____ ⋮ _____

96F _____ ⋮ _____

96G _____ ⋮ _____

96H _____ ⋮ _____

96I _____ ⋮ _____

96J _____ ⋮ _____

96K _____ ⋮ _____

96L _____ ⋮ _____

96M _____ ⋮ _____

96N _____ ⋮ _____

96O _____ ⋮ _____

96P _____ ⋮ _____

96Q _____ ⋮ _____

96R _____ ⋮ _____

96S _____ ⋮ _____

96T _____ ⋮ _____

96U _____ ⋮ _____

96V _____ ⋮ _____

☐ Continued on next page
☐ Continued on page _____
☐ End

‖ 96

Date: _____   Reference: _____

Title: _____

Ref. Line

97A _____ : _____

97B _____ : _____

97C _____ : _____

97D _____ : _____

97E _____ : _____

97F _____ : _____

97G _____ : _____

97H _____ : _____

97I _____ : _____

97J _____ : _____

97K _____ : _____

97L _____ : _____

97M _____ : _____

97N _____ : _____

97O _____ : _____

97P _____ : _____

97Q _____ : _____

97R _____ : _____

97S _____ : _____

97T _____ : _____

97U _____ : _____

97V _____ : _____

☐ Continued on next page
☐ Continued on page _____
☐ End

Date: _____   Reference: _____

Title: _____

Ref. Line

98A _____ : _____

98B _____ : _____

98C _____ : _____

98D _____ : _____

98E _____ : _____

98F _____ : _____

98G _____ : _____

98H _____ : _____

98I _____ : _____

98J _____ : _____

98K _____ : _____

98L _____ : _____

98M _____ : _____

98N _____ : _____

98O _____ : _____

98P _____ : _____

98Q _____ : _____

98R _____ : _____

98S _____ : _____

98T _____ : _____

98U _____ : _____

98V _____ : _____

☐ Continued on next page
☐ Continued on page _____
☐ End

‖ 98

Date: _____ Reference: _____

Title: _____

Ref. Line

99A _____ :_____

99B _____ :_____

99C _____ :_____

99D _____ :_____

99E _____ :_____

99F _____ :_____

99G _____ :_____

99H _____ :_____

99I _____ :_____

99J _____ :_____

99K _____ :_____

99L _____ :_____

99M _____ :_____

99N _____ :_____

99O _____ :_____

99P _____ :_____

99Q _____ :_____

99R _____ :_____

99S _____ :_____

99T _____ :_____

99U _____ :_____

99V _____ :_____

☐ Continued on next page
☐ Continued on page _____
☐ End

Date: _____   Reference: _____

Title: _____

Ref. Line

100A _____ :_____

100B _____ :_____

100C _____ :_____

100D _____ :_____

100E _____ :_____

100F _____ :_____

100G _____ :_____

100H _____ :_____

100I _____ :_____

100J _____ :_____

100K _____ :_____

100L _____ :_____

100M _____ :_____

100N _____ :_____

100O _____ :_____

100P _____ :_____

100Q _____ :_____

100R _____ :_____

100S _____ :_____

100T _____ :_____

100U _____ :_____

100V _____ :_____

☐ Continued on next page
☐ Continued on page _____
☐ End